# The Transforma Housewoкk

## Ben Bushill

# www.capallbann.co.uk

# The Transformation of Housework

Cover and internal illustrations by Ben Bushill
Cover design by Paul Mason

Published by:

Capall Bann Publishing
Auton Farm
Milverton
Somerset
TA4 1NE

# The Transformation of Housework

Energy surrounds you, fills you
You breathe it in with the air
You move through it and into it
with every  step of your life.

It is in your tasks, your housework
The chores you take for granted
In every movement that you make

Open your eyes
Open your heart
Slow down and touch the infinite

Return to your home
To the gentle smile inside
It is here now
You need only learn to listen

Listen
Hear
Feel
Love
Grow

# Contents

# Introduction

## Start to fall in love with your Housework

# I can Enjoy Housework??

OK lets face it, most of us hate housework, or at least find it something of a trial. Finding the time and the energy to tidy the house, clear up someone else's mess or clean the oven is not easy. One thing about housework is that there never seems to be a lot of time for it, it is often a case of squeezing in tasks when time allows, how then can we enjoy housework when we are always in a rush?

A meditation on the washing up seems like mission impossible, surely meditations take a long time. How can you take the time to melt into the warmth of the bubbles, play with the water and float away on a boat made of dirty dishes when the kids are swinging on your jumper, the toast is burning and you've got to be at work in 5 minutes???

Isn't there a danger of standing there, hands in the sink, water overflowing around your feet with a blissful smile on your face lost in your own world of watery caresses while the rest of the house falls to pieces around your ears?

Won't the neighbours think it strange when they glance through the window and see you dancing the light fantastic with the Vacuum. Will the rest of the family be convinced that you've totally flipped your lid if they come home and find you cuddling the dustpan and brush?

I'm afraid the answer is probably, yes.

But who is the crazy one, the person who moans and groans through their housework and finishes with a bad back as well as a bad attitude or you with a big smile on your face and energy tingling in your body?

Nobody expects us to enjoy our 'chores'. Not many folk smile happily when they clean the nasty sticky bits off the toilet

bowl. But don't panic! Enjoying your housework doesn't have to mean that your house has to become an untouchable shrine, or that you have to take 3 hours to dust the mantelpiece, you can find joy in your job and still do it quickly and avoid looking totally mad.

To tune into a task and enjoy you do not have to take a long time about it, nor does the task have to be done with intricate slowness. It takes only seconds to change your perspective, to alter your attitude just enough so that what you are doing becomes a positive experience, rather than an exercise in resentment and grumpiness.

If we take washing up for example, as you stand there by the sink, consciously relax your body and feel yourself sink down into your feet. Your shoulders are relaxed and open and your head is upright. Let the warmth of the water cradle your hands. Release any tension in your hands into the water, they are gently being massaged by the water and the bubbles. Just for a moment feel that you are not there to complete a job, but simply to feel calm and good. Let a feeling of stillness and energy fill your body. You are open, you are calm. You can enjoy where you are and what you are doing.

Just taking this short time to tune into yourself before you begin any task will make the difference between feeling better or worse at the end of the task. If you chose to let the job tire you, then tire you it will. If you chose to feel good then even doing hard work can be energising. Take one minute of stillness at the beginning of your next job and feel the difference even this short time will make. If you are doing twenty different things that day then that is twenty whole minutes of calmness you have given yourself! Wow! Who says we have no time for ourselves these days. You'll be surprised how good it feels (and how strange) to simply stop doing even for one single minute and just to be, not to do.

How would you rather feel?

# Eternal Housework

Leave behind your old perceptions of your everyday jobs and discover something fresh and new.

Before enlightenment, chop wood, carry water.
After enlightenment, chop wood, carry water.

The most obvious interpretation of this ancient quote is that these tasks will always be with us no matter what our stage of development. Lets have a modern version.

Before enlightenment, vacuum carpet, wash up dishes.
After enlightenment, vacuum carpet, wash up dishes.

Our tasks will always be there, no matter where we are in our lives, how rich, how poor, how focused or how distracted. How we carry out those tasks is up to us. During the course of our lives we will give countless hours to the mundane task. If your life is precious to you, why waste it in resented action that drains the energy of the body and deadens the mind?

So maybe there is more to the interpretation of this Zen wisdom than there first appears. Is it possible that the enlightenment is within the task, that real learning can come from and during the seemingly menial work we do. Why wait until the 'chores' are done when there is learning to be had all along the way. It is a tragic mistake to treat our daily tasks as things to 'get out of the way' and to ignore the objects that cross our paths in these tasks as unimportant and unrelated to us in any way. We rush through the jobs that make up a large proportion of our lives in order to get somewhere, to have the time to do something more fun, more interesting, more inspiring.

When you slow down enough to listen to the task, to the swish of the broom, the tinkle of water on the dish, then you will see that there is learning there, that everything that there is to know is within that task.

*'To see a world in a grain of sand,*
*and heaven in a wild flower'* - William Blake

The image of a DNA spiral and of a spiral galaxy return to me. They are exactly the same shape, a mirror of each other and yet one is unimaginably huge and the other the tiniest building block of life. Everything is within everything else. The ocean is in the fish as much as the fish is in the ocean. Can we find the beauty in the mundane ?

The small task is as important as the large, within even the simplest action is the potential for great learning, great joy.

If there is peace to be found in sitting by a river, or listening to the sea then there is also enlightenment in the gurgle of water in the sink, in the washing up. Countless sages have sat with nature and let the universe teach them, that same learning is in everything. In every household task, in the mop, the broom, the sink.

And as the river flows eternally onward so the tasks of the house repeat themselves, never ending. A stream of housework that will always stretch on into the future. We have the choice to hold ourselves back from this constant demand and to give into it with ill grace and grudging energy or to welcome what will be into our lives and treat housework as valuable time, as a time for peace and learning. Housework returns rhythmically, tasks repeat themselves. This will never change, there will never be a time when all the work is done and we can just rest. As night follows day, as the seasons change and return so our tasks will also be cyclic. There are cycles within all things, within the earth, within the body, how could the house be any different?

There is beauty in the mundane, it is undeniably there, we need only step sideways to see it.

When we think that we know a task, an action, we kill it. When you've washed the floor a thousand times the consciousness disappears, it is just another time. Yet we can slow down and find newness behind the familiarity. A simple movement of the hand, a wave, a gesture - performed a million times but when we slow down our awareness and move from a calm place, move as though it is the first and last movement that we will ever make, then it flowers like Spring's roses, the heart blooms and opens. It is possible to destroy the familiarity and the contempt that comes with it.

So how?? The chapters that follow will show you how to slow down and create an amazing space inside you and inside your home. Use the exercises, read the poems, feel the energy of the pictures and you will start to sense that there is a world of possibility waiting for you in your everyday jobs about the house!

# Transforming your Feeling

# When to Save and When to Spend

*Creating a Beautiful Revitalising Space in your Life.*

On one level the principle of conserving and spending is simply about learning to find the balance between the yang, active spending of energy and the yin, restful conserving of energy. When we work too hard and become tired and aching then we know we have been spending too much, working too hard without sufficient time for gentle rest and recovery. The active side has outstripped the passive side and we have lost balance.

This principle of saving and spending can also be about finding your connection with the tantien and discovering that movement can be effortless. As water flows in a stream, or as a plant grows, we too can move without effort. You move with all muscles relaxed and fluid, all joints loose and freely connecting. When we connect our movements to the sea of energy that is in the tantien then every movement can become as graceful and effortless as a bird soaring on the breeze. We are saving as we are spending when we move like this.

So these two parts of the principle come together and we find a non-judgemental acceptance of what we are doing and how we are doing it so that everything can change. Housework and chores become a chance to tune into the chi energy that is all around us. When we stop judging the job we are doing as boring or dirty then it can become like an exercise, a meditation, a way to touch the infinite. A chance to slow down

**15**

Mopping can be a joyful experience when we learn how to connect to the tantien centre!

enough to truly listen to life and ourselves. And this is when the chi starts to come, when you will feel energy dancing about your hands, your head, your whole body.

And then we discover that there can be a relationship between us and the tool that we are using for our housework. When we touch the energy we are given a means to communicate with and to listen to all that surrounds us. There is a oneness, not only with the tools we use but also with the dirt, with the floor, with the bathroom sink. When you work from this sensation and sure feeling of oneness then every action every spending of energy is also a way to conserve and build chi. Moving in this awareness can change everything we do into a way to grow ourselves, to conserve and feel the chi circulating around our bodies and hearts.

Well, you may say, that all sounds very nice and lovely but how do I do it, how do I plug in to all this wonderful, revitalising, exciting energy (especially when I've got ten thousand shirts to iron, a mountain of washing up and the cat's just been sick on the carpet).

What is to follow will show you how, how make it a reality. Use the simple exercises in the book and discover a new relationship with your chores!

**Goodbye backache!** - *learning how to move with your housework.*

So what if the energy and satisfaction of doing a job came not from the completion of the task, but from the task itself, from the movement and awareness of connections? Connections in your own body and connections with the tools you use and the things that you clean.

Is it possible to turn housework into a dance, an exercise for health and a way to create, rather than expend energy?

It is possible but first we have to have the humility to learn to move again, we have to go right back to the beginning and become like a baby taking it's first steps. Like the baby we accept that we don't know how, and like the baby we don't judge ourselves harshly if sometimes our steps are faltering and uncertain.

## The Tantien

*Connecting to the belly centre.*

Stand with your feet shoulder width apart and parallel. Relax and drop your shoulders, feel your weight really sinking into your feet and into the ground beneath you. Allow there to be space under your armpits, all your joints are soft. Imagine that there is a golden thread attached to the very top of your head and that it is gently lifting you upwards.

Pause in this position and feel the stillness. If your body moves slightly, maybe rocking from side to side then just allow it to do so. Stand like a tree, rooted in the ground and yet gently moving.

Slowly bring both palms to your Tantien a point about 2 inches below the navel. This is your belly centre, it is from here that you will start to enjoy your housework.

## Shifting your Weight

To begin with just practice moving your weight without anything in your hands.Stand as you were in the previous exercise, feet shoulder width apart, shoulders relaxed, knees slightly bent.

Then turn and open your left foot so that it is at an angle of about 90 degrees to your other foot. Turn your body to face in the direction of the left foot.

Slowly shift your weight forwards into your left foot until all your weight rests in that foot. Keep your focus on your tantien, the belly centre leads the rest of the body.

Then at the same slow pace allow your weight to sink back into the right foot. Concentrate on the feeling of the tantien moving and everything else moving with it.

Really slow down the movement, feel your feet beneath you and let your mind be calm. Imagine you are moving through water or that the air is thick and alive about you.

You can take this same movement and feeling with you into your housework. The most obvious application is when you are vacuuming, mopping or sweeping. Move your tantien when you move the vacuum or the mop, not just your shoulders. It is so easy to be lost in a train of thought when you are doing simple tasks like these that you have done a thousand times before. Take a chance! take a fresh look at what you are doing and how you are moving. You might surprise yourself and enjoy what you are doing! It is in that enjoyment and that freshness that you will find the energy to rejuvenate yourself and clean your inner house at the same time as you clean your carpet.

Move with your vacuum, dance with your vacuum. Let your shoulders be relaxed. Your tantien moves your arms, your elbows connect to your tantien. Feel the energy circulate in your body as you move. It is as though the vacuum were an extension of you, connected to you, not some heavy beast that you have to lug around the floor.

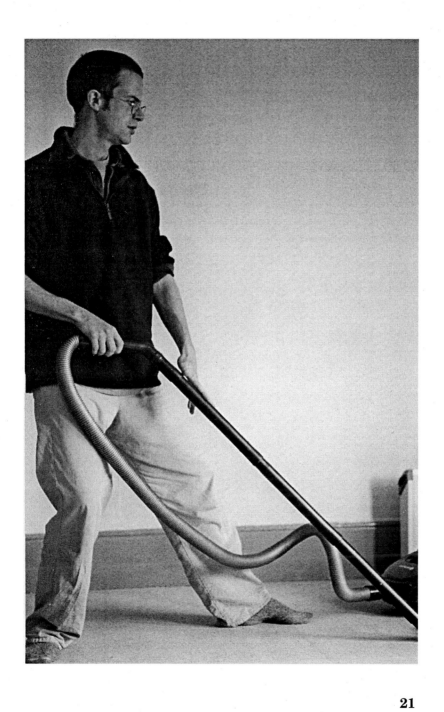

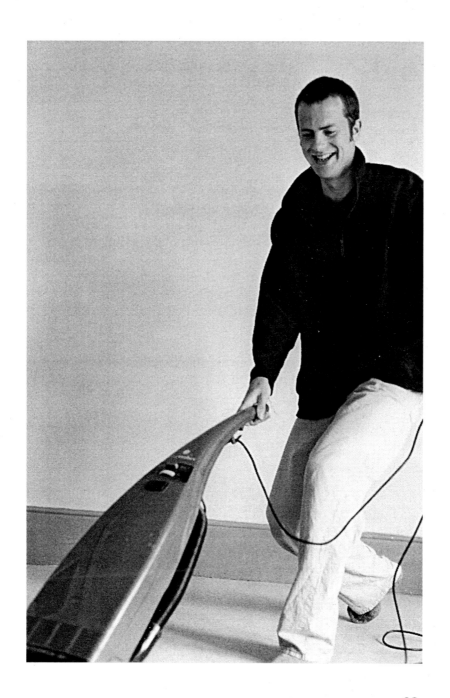

Imagine you are dancing with a sexy woman or man as you vacuum, how would you move, how would you dance then?

# Plugging In!

*Diving into the chi energy*

Before you read this page ask yourself this simple question. Am I ready to suspend cynicism and everything I think I know about moving and about housework?

OK so maybe its not such a simple question but ask it anyway, if the answer is yes or even maybe then you are almost there already. If you can let go the feeling of housework being a must do and just connect purely to the movement then you can learn how to plug in!

Before you start a job for real, touch the chi. Take the movement that you will be using in your job and then slow it down. Really slow it down so that you are moving incredibly slowly.

Take the movement of washing a dish for example, one hand holding the plate and the other gently circling an imaginary scourer.

Your body moves from the tantien, and each millimetre of movement is important. Move as though you are moving through water, let all the hardness in your body melt into warmth and fluidity. Inside your body you are fluid, softly moving smooth parts. The fluid way is the natural way to move, every cell in your body is trying to show the way to be in the fluidity. You are a being of effortless movement. Every part of your body is moving infinitesimally, if any part feels achy or stuck feel gentle movement come to that part and release the tightness.

You may feel a warmth in your palms or a tingling feeling about your hands and your body. Melt into that feeling, let go of your thoughts and gently feel yourself soften into the energy. The more you let go the more chi energy you will feel.

Don't think about how you will apply the movement to real life, let go of the idea of the movement as housework and move for movements sake, to touch the chi, you are moving purely to feel joy and energy, no other reason matters.

When you begin to feel the chi then you can take that same movement and speed it up, apply it to the real business of housework. With time and practice you will be able to turn every task into an opportunity to tune in and conserve energy.

Next time you begin a job take 5 minutes to try this exercise. Move with the chi, plug in before you start and that same awareness will accompany you into your action.

# Slowing Down and Making Space

*How to listen to the stillness inside*

It is all too easy to charge into a task with a feeling of urgency or hurriedness taking the pressures of the day with you into what you are doing. When we move like this, quickly and without attention to where we are or what we are doing in the moment then we lose that most precious gift, awareness. It is awareness that can change a task from something boring and repetitive into an enriching experience.

So how do we find and keep this awareness?

To find a connection with the energy in the task and to feel connected to the tools and objects that we use we have to slow down the mind. The mind can be like a restless child jumping from one thought to another. First you are thinking about the messy front room, then you find yourself thinking about what you are going to have for dinner, when your mum's birthday is or who won the battle of Hastings. Sometimes there seems to be no reason to the mind, it is as though it has a life of it's own and the last thing it wants to do is really focus on what it is that the rest of you is doing. It seems as though the mind and it's thoughts are travelling at about a thousand miles an hour!

But you can slow down the mind. You can find the spaces in between your thoughts. It is in that space that you will find a real connection to your true self and to whatever it is that you are doing.

Find some time when you are not going to be disturbed by anyone. Sit in an upright, comfortable position, either on the floor or on a firm chair. Allow the body to relax without slumping. You are aiming for a position of relaxed attention. Rest your hands on your knees and feel your shoulders sink

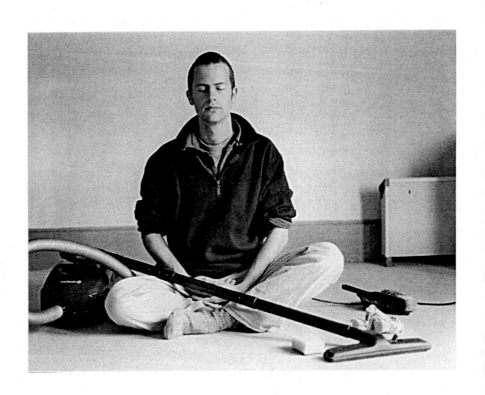

down and the tension release from your arms and neck. Let your chest feel open and loose, your head balances on your neck without effort or strain as though a golden cord is attached to the top of your head and is gently lifting you towards the ceiling. You can do this right now as you are reading this book, take this opportunity to slow down and listen to yourself and your heart.

Let your focus come to your breath. The breath comes in, feel the lungs expand gently without forcing, a sense of energy is filling you, flowing from your lungs to the rest of your body. Gently listen to the mind, thank it for all it's hard work and then ask it to just listen for a little while. Any thoughts that come let them float away as if on a river, don't give them your attention, let them come and go with no judgement or criticism.

There is space between those thoughts right now. Hear the silence in the spaces between the thoughts, between your breaths.

Everything is slowing down, the breath is slow and even, the mind is calm, gently listening. Be with this wonderful sense of space. Feel what it means to be alive, to have a body, to have a heart. In the silence you can hear your heart beating, you are alive, truly alive.

Now take this feeling, this awareness with you into your work, into you interaction with the objects of housework. Listen to the vacuum, the dustpan and brush, really feel the water in the sink. From this place of silence you can build a new relationship with housework. Right now you are reinventing housework. You are doing something that has never been done before. It is possible to feel joy in what you are doing. As unlikely as it may seem there is real inspiration in those simple jobs that we do every day without thinking. *Without thinking.* With feeling.

At first the feeling of silence and calmness may be fleeting and difficult to find. But with patience and just a few minutes every day you can start to carry this sense of space with you. In the beginning it may take a long time to tune in, to find this calm place but with practice you will find it easier and easier to slow down. Just taking one single, precious minute before beginning your job can be enough to transform 'a dirty job that someone's got to do' into the chance to feel a joyful sense of connection with your surroundings and to feel rejuvenating energy tingling in your body.

## The House and the Body

So, why do housework? Maybe it is better just to do the barest minimum and save a lot of unnecessary effort. What is the motivation for keeping your house in a good order? It comes down to our connection with the place in which we live. Do you love your house? Taking care of that which we love is a pleasure not a chore, so lets nurture that sense of respect and love.

It is possible to feel truly connected to your house as it is possible to feel connected to the tasks around the house. Indeed to feel good about the work that you are doing in the house and to enjoy your housework you must first enjoy and feel grateful to the house that you are living in and maintaining. When we feel connected to where we live it brings a sense of wholeness to our lives. Whether you live in a bedsit or a country manor the feeling is the same.

I find it very useful to connect the house with the body to encourage this sense of respect. In many ways the house and the body fulfil similar functions. The body houses our mind, our spirit, our heart. It is the essential, indispensable home of our consciousness. The smooth function and happiness of the body and it's organs is crucial for our overall well-being. When one part of our body ceases to function as it should we very quickly feel the consequences. Even something seemingly minor, like a small muscle strain can affect the function of the whole and make life extremely difficult and uncomfortable and when a major part of us, such as an organ, is ailing our world is turned upside down and everything changes.

The house, our home, contains this wonderful, complex, beautiful organism that is us within it. If the body houses the consciousness then it is our home that houses our body. For the smooth running of the internal environment of our body we must take care of the external environment in which we spend so much of our time. The house is a natural extension of our body.

Different rooms connect to different parts of the body, to different organs. Most houses start with a hallway. The door opens and we exchange with our environment, air and energy move in and out just as they do through our mouth and nose. The passageways and corridors of the house then are like the lungs and passageways of the body allowing the free passage of air and energy in and out and circulating it to the rooms of the house, letting fresh clean energy permeate every room. When we keep the hallways, stairs and corridors free of obstruction we are keeping the bronchioles and arteries free flowing and healthy. Even food comes in through the front door, moving down the oesophagus/hallway to the kitchen for digestion.

So to the kitchen. Often considered to be the centre of a house, traditionally the hearth and the fire were very much the focus of the household. They held this place of importance because it is here that the food is prepared, that nourishment is passed to the people living there. The kitchen is the stomach, the digestion of the house. Raw food is transformed into a form that is useful to the body, we take our nourishment here, much of our health and energy stems from the kitchen. So keep the kitchen in good health, keep it clean and uncluttered so that digestion can take place as effortlessly as possible.

The lounge and the bedroom I connect to the heart. In these rooms we find our quiet space. Here we relax and revive ourselves, retreat from the pressures of the day. As the heart of the body is a place of rest and peace so the heart of the house can act in the same way. We are free here, away from work and confrontations, able to return to who we really are, to return to the heart. When you come home after a difficult day there is nothing better than finding safe relaxing space in your lounge or on your bed. When you want to free the mind and the spirit, to calm yourself on a deep level, you must return to the heart. The heart welcomes you back without judgement, just as your lounge or you bedroom welcome and comfort you.

And so to the bathroom. *Essential* to the house allowing the free flow of water in and out of the house (and the body!). The kidneys and the large intestine both do their wonderful work in this room. The bathroom, the kidneys of the house, is responsible for letting go the waste products of life. Those things that we really don't want inside our bodies or inside our houses any more. In the bathroom we refresh ourselves, wash away the days dirt and grime and emerge clean and new just as the kidneys clean and filter our blood, granting us new life.

And here you are in the middle of this complex organism the home. You are the immune system of the body. Moving from room to room keeping everything running smoothly, allowing new energy in, removing the old. Your housework stops illness and blockages manifesting in the body. Your day to day tasks, washing up, cleaning, vacuuming are the processes of the body that must happen regularly for it to live. Your house is a living thing and you are keeping it healthy.

**32**

To be healthy in heart, body, mind and spirit what surrounds you must also be healthy. Feel that as you perform your household tasks you are caring for an extension of your body. When you feel the connection of the bathroom to the kidneys for example, a new sacredness comes into your interaction through housework. Imagine you are moving around your kidney, returning each cell to healthy function. As you clean the sink you are cleaning yourself.

Allow a new gentleness to come into your work. When you touch the parts of your house with gentleness and respect that respect is reflected right back to you. Compare how you feel after scrubbing at the bath franticly or grudgingly and then how you feel when you clean as if you are cleaning something very precious (and what could be more precious than you internal organs). The way you act in the world comes right back to you. When you approach the world and your work with gentleness and care then these qualities will manifest in your life.

There is a fast and definite way to prove this to yourself. Clean the mirror! See what is reflected back to you. Is it the calm gentle face of someone loving what the are doing and where they live?

"This world is like a mirror, reflect on what you do,
and if you face it smiling, it will smile right back to you"
*Culture*

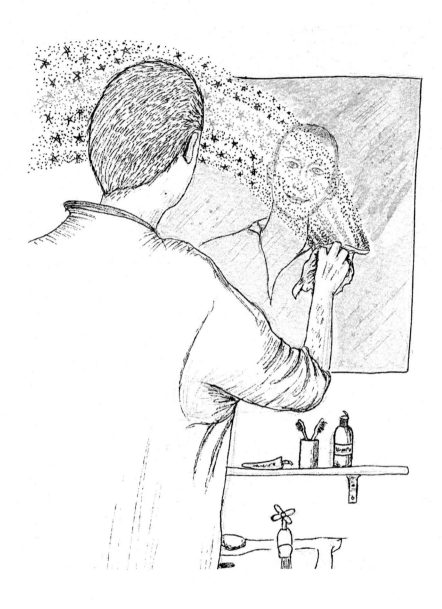

# A Short Exercise in Respect

Love your organs and love your house. As you tidy your home you are moving through your body. Each thing that you touch is a part of you. Touch each part with the utmost care. It is as though you are reaching into your body and touching your heart or your kidney. You are returning your house to vibrant health right now.

As your house breathes, you breath. You are returning to vibrant health. As you work gently on each room you are working on yourself.

Feel the energy in your body that comes with gentleness. As you reach out to clean feel yourself becoming cleansed, renewed, refreshed. Every movement through the house is a return to gentleness. Every part that you touch is touched with love. What an opportunity to fill your home with loving energy. Everything that you touch receives this energy. All the rooms of the house are filled with light and love.

What a place to come home to. Somewhere where everything that you have touched carries the echo of love. Your energy is in all the house, in all the objects of the house. You are surrounded by beautiful loving energy. The energy fills you and lifts you. You are revitalised. Tingling energy is everywhere it fills your house and your heart.

Return to the way of gentleness for it is here that you will heal your wounds. Househealing. Bodyhealing. Lifehealing.

# As Within so Without

What would you do if you can stand now,
right inside your body?
would you rush around and poke and prod,
and do everything real shoddy?
or would you hold and touch with gentle care,
and not just quickly squander,
the chance to feel and love your organs
with a sense of wonder.
For wonderful they are
and in their wonder humble,
yet without them all your dreams would fall
and edifices tumble.
Come ponder then a moment
and think about the chance
that what you do inside your house
could possibly enhance
the way in which your life will feel,
within you and without.
If you move and flow with gentle care
there really is no doubt
that your organs will be happy too,
Kidney, heart and spleen
Gall bladder, lung and liver
all will be serene
now touch your house
with all the same respect that you would give
to blood and bone
your organs home, allowing you to live..

# Are You Really Here?

*Being Present and the Infinite Trickiness of the Mind.*

Where are you when you are cleaning the bath? Are you really here when you are washing the floor? Many times I am sure the answer is that you are only partially here. Your body is there gaily going through the physical motions of performing your job, whatever it may be, but your mind is wandering off somewhere, perhaps contemplating what you might cook for tea, what chore you will do next, or how come the kids always forget to wipe their feet when they come in. The mind has a 'wonderful' (or wanderful) tendency to always be moving a little bit faster than the rest of us and while the mind and our thoughts have such a strong influence over us we tend to follow them, drawn from what we are doing into a possible future or a remembered past. Even when the mind is away in some beautiful fantasy world, lying on a beach pinnocolada in hand it is still taking us away from where we really are.

Well, you may say, I'd rather be lying on the beach sipping cocktails than be down on my knees scrubbing the back of the oven. Perfectly understandable of course only not really possible, the imagination might be there but the rest of you, most of you, your body, heart and spirit are still very much in the kitchen.

So why be here now? Why be fully present with whatever it is that you are doing?

Just consider for a moment how many times you really are fully present with what you are doing during the day. When you are driving the car perhaps or when you first wake up in the morning. When you are cleaning your teeth or when you are arriving at work. If you are totally honest with yourself you may well see that you are never fully with what you are doing but that most of the time you are listening to the ever busy mind that is chattering on about your day to come or how much better it was yesterday. Our thoughts never stop throughout the day and they can suck us away with them into an imagined past or future. Yet it is in this moment, and this moment and this moment that we are alive, that the miracle of life and breath is passing through us, that we can feel wonderfully, beautifully and completely present, unfortunately thanks to our thoughts we are not usually here to experience it. Great chunks of our lives are lost to us. Gone. That breath you just took will never come again. And nor will that one. Wouldn't it be a good idea to really enjoy them? To really feel your life as it passes through your body.

I went to the doctor's the other day and was shocked to find that I only have between about forty and sixty years to live. Apparently, as I'm twenty eight now and a normal human being, death will be coming along in a while and there aren't any anti-biotics to stop it. Blimey! I had better see about making the most of it. Now my thoughts come in, well then win the lottery quick, buy a holiday to the Caribbean, go and get drunk, blah, blah, blah. Do this then you'll be happy, buy this then you'll be happy, just finish the ironing and then sit down and then you'll be happy.

Its clever you see, your mind. Always promises. Promising you that you'll feel happy, fulfilled or content when you have just done this thing or that thing or that if it could only be how it was last year then everything would be OK and you would be happy.

But maybe it is much more simple than our thoughts lead us to believe.

Maybe happiness and peace are here right now. Right now whatever you are doing, whether it be pinnocolada sipping or oven cleaning. The happiest people I know are the ones who have had the least practice at it. The ones who haven't been around long enough to feel jaded, to feel as if they know everything. The children. My friend James (age 6) helped me with the washing up the other day. Watching him discover the sink and the soapy water was an education. Whilst there was a part of me that cringed slightly over time another gallon of water ended up on the floor instead of in the sink, his joy in the job was infectious. He was totally there with what he was doing. He wasn't thinking about what he would do next he was just washing up. All of him, his heart, body, mind and spirit. And that is where the energy is. Where chi is. Where happiness is. Where vitality is. In this moment called now.

Now is always with us. When we are vacuuming the floor, when we are cleaning the toilet, when we are relaxing in the armchair it is there, but we have to choose to feel it. Can we have the child's mind, the beginner's mind. We all did once and we can all find it again.

One way to learn is to slow down, to be aware of what you are doing. To feel, not to think. Let your awareness rest in your hands, what do they feel as they touch the objects around the house, what is the bare sensation. The feeling not the interpretation of the feeling. Practice the slowing down exercise on page 26 before you begin your chore. Let the mind slow down and give some space to the feeling and the experience.

It is no instant process, the mind will not suddenly stop, say 'OK I'll be nice and quiet for a while'. Your thoughts will keep coming, but you have the choice of whether to follow them or not. Just watch what arises and come back to the feeling. One of the thoughts that will arise is of course 'right I've got to be in the moment, I must stop thinking' which is of course a thought in itself (you see how tricky the mind is? and that's nothing) just watch it come and then come back to the feeling, back to the simplicity of what is happening, what you are feeling right now.

You may just get a glimpse of what it means to be truly present. And then you will start to feel the energy that is all around you. Then you will be really living and each of those precious breaths that fill our lives will be felt and appreciated.

# Chores! Wonderful Chores!

# Singing with your Sink

*Melt into the world of watery caresses*

Do you want to feel like this when your are doing your washing up? When you approach your work with that 'oh no I've got to...' feeling you are pretty much turning yourself into this chap, does he look as if his internal organs are happy? What you feel *will* directly affect what is happening inside of you.

But this works both ways! When you feel peaceful, happy and accepting, that also goes inside to directly influence your organs!

A chance to do the washing up! Play with the water in the washing up bowl. Fill the bowl with water and watch it spill over the edges in glistening cascading waterfalls, relish the feeling of warmth on your hands. Take joy in the bubbles that gently touch your skin. This is water therapy, not washing up.

This is a chance to soothe your hands and your whole body. Imagine that your hand reflects your whole body, you are within your hand, you are diving into the water, you are immersed in it, kissed, washed, soothed. The dishes are your playthings, the scourer the yin yang scourer  is a joy to use (such a mirror for ourselves the harshness and the softness). And the dishes are transformed!

Enjoy the transformation, within it is your own.

Feel the movement of washing the dishes, the scrubbing circle, the ever present circle another life mirror. Relax the shoulders release the wrists, the movement flows from the tantien. The weight shifts in my feet as I reach to leave the clean plates to one side.

Nothing bothers me, the flow of my life in that ten minutes is absolutely crystal clear. The job has a beginning and an end, it is perfectly achievable. In this life where nothing is certain, where we question ourselves constantly, when we are continually bombarded by challenges and difficulties, that simple, that beautifully simple, familiar task takes away the worries of the future and the regrets of the past. It drowns out children, parents, television - dive in, let go the mundane and bliss out in the achievable, easy and beautiful task of washing the dishes.

Who says we never get time for ourselves these days? That we are always too busy. Perhaps we are looking in the wrong places for time and relaxation. Look within the busy-ness. Take a fresh look at the time that can open up where there seemed to be none.

There is always time for love and energy in your day!

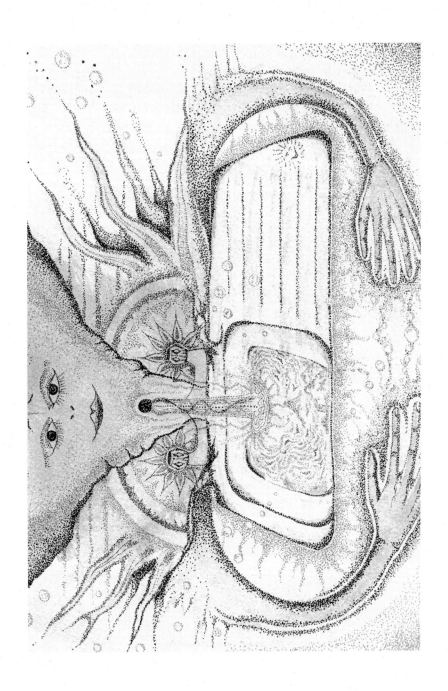

# The Sink

Mirror well, you mirror well
All that I bring to you
Plunge pool fountains end
Clean and clear and crisp
You break the light with silvery whispers

You carry the infinite within
Water, that knows all
Life's sire
Silver servant who bears the water
I am refreshed by you
By the light you carry,
By the beauty of steel,
Of metal.

Bubbles dance their whirlpool crystal spiral
And you lend light to their dance
And wait
To refresh and renew again
Softness and steel,
Allies and friends

I bathe my hands inside you
Cradled in blue
All is clear
All is clean
My dishes
My hands
My heart.


Thank you sink for your clarity and the rare and precious
blue crystal light that dances inside you. A rich gift indeed.

When I look upon you with the eyes of a child, with the eyes of wonder, I see a thousand diamond reflections, silver waterfalls.

What a gift to look with freshness at what we think we know.

## The Surface Clean and the Deep Down Shine!

*How to deal  with your inner dirt*

Have you noticed how frustrated shop assistants smile at you?

It is seldom a smile that lights up their face and really makes your day. It appears and disappears in seconds, you get a brief flash of teeth, a tiny crinkling of the cheeks and then it is gone. They are not smiling from the inside, it just touches the surface.

Have you ever noticed how a kitchen looks when you do some of the washing up, and ignore the dirty cooker and the surfaces?

Are there any similarities here?

Companies are always on at us to use their products and find that deep down shine, to wipe away the grime in half the time or some other nonsense. But what is the deep down shine? I think it is something that most frustrated shop assistants have lost track of.

I cleaned my bathroom the other day. When I started it didn't look too bad, the sink was a bit a grubby and the floor needed a vacuum but as I got into it I found more and more that needed doing. It felt as though the cleaning that had happened there had been very superficial, almost as if it was

covering up the real dirt not wiping it away. I found that the shower curtain had gone mouldy, the tile grout black and that all manner of interesting old grime had built up around the taps. So I rolled up my sleeves took a deep breath (and a brief pause to find the smile) and I went for it! Took a toothbrush to the tricky bits and a scourer to the tough bits. What was I looking for? Yup, you guessed it, the deep down shine.

I found it! When I finished the bathroom looked different, it wasn't completely obvious how and why, but it had a freshness and a feeling that were good to be with. All of it was shining, all of it was smiling.

An old feeling came back to haunt me the other day. Something came up from the past and wobbled my self confidence, made me feel nervous and unsure. Something that I thought I had dealt with at the time but which I only glossed over. Surface cleaned.

So I got to work with the scourer of my awareness. Found some interesting old grime that had built up around the place, and realised that I had never really looked at it, just pretended it wasn't there.

How do you clean inside? How do you find the deep down shine for yourself as well as your bathroom?

With gentleness, with patience, with light. First you have to see, to take courage and to look deep enough to realise that there are crusty bits stuck around your inner taps. Don't be overwhelmed by them, and start feeling that because you have got a few crusty bits you are not a worthwhile person or that all you have are the not so pleasant bits. Everyone has their dark corners, we either go for the surface clean and pretty much ignore them or we let the light in and let them go.

So find some quiet time, and look, you don't need to go digging around in your psyche looking for ghosts, just deal with the ones that come up. Usually there are plenty, I know I have no shortage. When a feeling comes up don't run from it. Allow it to rise into your awareness.

If you are feeling nervous for example, just stay with the nervousness, tune in to what it feels like in your body and in your heart. Picture what the nervous you looks like. Let go of any feelings of judgement. Don't give yourself a hard time about feeling nervous, or think you should not feel that way. That self judgement will only add to the negative feelings. If you catch yourself thinking 'oh God, I feel nervous, I shouldn't be feeling nervous' then slow down and say to yourself in a gentle inner voice 'it is really ok to feel what you are feeling'

Allow your feelings to be. Look at them with gentle inner eyes. Feel what the nervous part of you needs, if he wants reassurance that it is ok for him to be that way then offer that reassurance. Give space and light to the part that feels dark.

Give yourself the space to feel. To feel without judgement, with only the all accepting love of your heart.

When you do this, when you allow the dark to be there, you will find that it is no longer so dark, sometimes all that part of you needs is to be acknowledged. Trust yourself to get into the dark corners of your inner house and you can find that deep down shine.

When you shine from inside your whole face smiles, your eyes, your teeth, your hair. Just like that bathroom, you and everyone around you will really see and feel the difference.

Hold yourself with kindness and gentleness and smiles that rise from a place deep inside will grace your face and bring light to other peoples dark corners.

# Down and Dirty

*Accepting the darkness in your house and in your life and finding a new balance...*

Sometimes you will have to get down and dirty in the housework stakes. Maybe your sink has been leaking just a little bit and all the bottles of assorted cleaning fluids, brush cleaners and old J-cloths are getting smelly and there is a layer of furry mould growing over everything inside. Shit happens. These are the kind of jobs that are oh so easy to put off.

Picture the scene, a Sunday morning, the sun is shining, you've just eaten a splendid breakfast and done those few dishes, you go to put away the washing up liquid and it is there.....

That cupboard with the mould that you have been only half looking at for about three weeks, scared to look too closely because you know what that will mean. Yes, you are going to have to get down and dirty. Inevitably these jobs are always low level, you have to be on your hands and knees, you have to get your face low down and close to the smelly job, and you are going to have to put your hands into that stuff. Pretty unappealing, down-right horrible some would say. Can you transform this experience? Can you find some light amongst the mould.

The job itself is wonderfully transforming. You are about to change this stinking, damp hole into a clean, bright and organised cupboard. You will probably find too that it is the starting that is difficult, it is the idea of having to do something that seems so nasty that makes the job difficult, once you actually get going at it and stop thinking the revulsion fades. So as with all tasks that we really don't want to do, the first part of the process is about shifting the concept that the job is going to be boring, grimy and unpleasant.

It helps to connect the task to yourself. If you can feel that you are cleansing part of yourself then suddenly the job is more worthwhile. Stop before you begin and reflect on something that is mouldy inside of you, either physically or emotionally. If you have any aches and pains in your body take a few seconds to tune into them and feel that you are getting inside that pain as you are cleaning those dirty corners. You are returning those parts of you that are not flowing smoothly to healthy function. As you wipe away the dirt feel yourself cleaned and your body becoming fresher.

Tune into a situation that is in your life, perhaps one that is difficult or ugly and you are unwilling to face. As you clean the cupboard feel that you are shedding light on that situation. Don't dwell on the dirt or hardship of the situation, there is always going to be dirt in your life as there are always going to be dirty jobs to do. If you only look at the dirt it is very easy for it to become overwhelming. Spending time with the dark and the mould and the ugliness will pretty quickly lead to you becoming bogged down in it and unable the see the light for all the dirt around you. Instead connect to the dirt and darkness, the real dirt of the job and the dirt in your life, feel it and see it without getting caught up in it and what it means.

You can be aware of the darkness in your life without having to dive into it and be overwhelmed by it.

Just touch it with your heart, feel it without thinking about it or judging it and then let the cleaning wipe it away. Let the light banish the darkness. We have to face these dark parts of ourselves but we don't have to dwell with them to do so. Touch them and acknowledge them as you acknowledge the dirt that needs to be removed as part of your housework, then wipe it away and let the sparkle come back.

It is often so tempting when we are faced by a difficult and overwhelming situation or by a problem that we cannot resolve, to go further into it, to think about it constantly in an attempt to understand it and bring clarity, but it will not help. When you see your dirty cupboard and recognise it as a problem do you sit down on the floor next to it and play will the grime and the mould?

Do you play with it, look at it from the left side and from the right side? No! because that is not helpful it will not help the cupboard get clean, just as turning a situation over and over in your head will not help you see the light that is there. Just wipe it away, wipe away the dirt and wipe away your troubles, make some space for the light to come in and your cupboard will be a happier place and so will you.

We cannot deny the dirt in our lives, that part will always be there. There will never come a time when everything smells of roses, when it never rains, when your life is trouble free. There will never come a time when the housework is finished when the washing up stays done, when the floor stays clean. These jobs, and the negatives in your life are always going to be around. So accept them. Accept that this is part of life, part of the wonderful balance of life and that without them, without the dirt, then the other could not be there either.

The darkness is inevitable, but don't cling on to it, don't dwell in it, don't bemoan the fact the you have got to clean the toilet again, accept it and move past it. Wipe away the dirt, let the hardships go and make space for the light. The more you think about pain the more painful it will become, the more you put off cleaning your mouldy cupboard the mouldier and smellier it will become. Wipe it away, don't stay with the dark. Touch it, acknowledge it, accept it, then let it go.

OK, so now your cupboard is clean, the carpet vacuumed and the surfaces sparkling. You are feeling great, on top of the

world, full of joy and vitality. The temptation now of course is to try to hang onto that feeling, that cleanliness. But I'm afraid this is just as impossible, just as destructive as seeing only the dirt. Where there is cleanliness there will come dirt, the opposite is always there even within the extreme. The more extreme, the closer the reverse. If your surfaces are totally spotless, polished to a high shine, even the slightest mark will seem like a pile of cow dung.

We must accept the cycle, the swing between the two extremes as it will continually happen. We have the choice whether to be caught up in that swing or simply to observe it and accept it. The same holds true of the feelings within us, when we try to hold onto one extreme or another, then the very act of trying to hold on will bring us down. We are doomed to fail. If we can acknowledge and truly accept the endlessness of the cycle of housework, that dirty will become clean, and that clean will become dirty, then we can accept that cycle within. Accept it and not be consumed by it, but allow it to be. As above, so below. As without, so within.

When we try to hold onto one of these states, if we try to hold onto happiness, then it becomes only a memory of happiness, a concept of the mind not a feeling. Only by letting it go, by realising the inevitability of change will you understand that happiness is not a memory of a feeling but a living experience that changes as everything around you changes. Love your housework and love life for the two are the same, they have the same pattern, move through the same extremes. Be in that point of balance that watches the changes roll in and accepts them as the beach accepts the waves.

When judgement is gone chores are no longer chores. When we cease to see the dirt as bad, we can quietly help the balance to return without resenting the labour.

As there is yin so there is yang, as there is dirty so there is clean.

As night, day. As winter, summer. As hot, cold. As life, death. This is an indisputable universal law, it is part of the balance of the universe. Housework, everyday jobs that we do so often, are as much a part of that rhythm as the elements of nature, as plants and animals, as humans. Let the flow of housework teach you about cycles, about opposites. All reality is reflected in your housework. Can you see it? Can you feel it?

## Night and Day, Within and Without

*Learning to Accept our Lives*

So our housework shows us Yin and Yang. The dirty and the clean, the dark and the light, the hard and the soft. Both sides will always exist, there will always be opposites within our lives. Our most wonderful teacher is of course the world around us. A world of extremes and contrasts, yet also a world of harmony. The mountain top, jagged rock and eagle's claw all exist alongside the softness of a spring morning, the first opening of a new flower and the gently flowing stream. We see no contradiction in these diverse parts of our planet. Yet sometimes when we find this diversity within ourselves, we recoil.

Our emotions, our thoughts and the physical feelings within our bodies all have the potential for extremes. Within us dwell feelings of sadness, vulnerability, loneliness but also joy, strength and love. Within us are thoughts full of compassion and kindness, yet we also think of aggression and violence. Within our bodies is the feeling of energy and vitality and also pain and exhaustion.

Opposites will always exist in our world and most of us wouldn't want it any other way. Would we choose to have antelopes but no lions, would the world be a better place if the weather was always warm and mild or would we miss the storms? And what of our internal world? is that any different? Do you dream of a life with only peace and happiness. What of pain, what of sadness?

The dream of a life without problems, without pain, is just that, a dream. To find a sense of fulfilment, of lasting contentment we must learn to accept the hurt as we eagerly accept the joy. If we can only feel and believe, truly believe, in our hearts, bodies, minds and spirits that both our dark side and our light side are an inevitable part of life, like the snow and the sun, like the clean and the dirty, then we can move toward a place of calm vitality, toward a sense of completeness.

When we sit in judgement of our lives we are missing that essential enjoyment and acceptance. If you wake in the morning look out of the window and think 'damn, its raining' or 'whoopee, its sunny' you are putting conditions on your enjoyment of life. When we learn to accept our external and our internal world for what it is then we can begin to love all of our lives, not just the 'nice' bits. If you wish away the negative and hunt for the positive you are denying half of your life.

For situations to change, for the pain to move, for the sadness to transform, we have to allow it to be. It is like making space around a feeling and giving it the chance to move and change. If we learn anything from our housework, from the never ending cycle of chores then it is that nothing is permanent, nothing stays clean. Likewise your negative feelings will change. Your positive feelings will change. The more you try and hold onto a happy feeling with your mind and your life, the more it slips away. If we can learn to take a step back, feel what we are feeling without judgement and without trying to cling onto it then it will change. Pain, like happiness will not last forever. Yin and Yang are in permanent movement each moving towards the other, the cleaner the house the closer is the opposite. The darker the feeling, the closer the light.

Accepting the darkness in our lives as we accept the light allows things to move and change, nothing becomes fixed and stagnant. When we accept a feeling, allow it to be without judgement or criticism, without an agenda then we give it the space to transform. By accepting all the feelings within us, by accepting our thoughts we are accepting life. Judgement is not ours to make. Life flows through us every day, every breath, if we have to decide what is good and what is bad then we are missing so much, denying so much. Life is passing, don't miss it!

Housework is a tremendous way to learn to accept our grimy bits, the darker side that maybe we don't want to look at. Accepting our mess, our rubbish is a wonderful tool to show us how to move and change. You can release your negative feelings as you release your rubbish. When we can accept the darkest parts of our houses then we are halfway to accepting the darkest parts of ourselves.
(After I wrote this I came home to find the cat had pooed very neatly in the middle of my bed. I laughed so much. I guess the universe was just checking that I had really learnt this lesson!)

## An Exercise in Internal Acceptance

Find some time when you can sit quietly without being disturbed. About 20 minutes would be a good amount of time to start with. You can sit on the floor or on a chair, however you are most comfortable. Allow yourself to come to calmness. Listen to your breath and feel your contact with the earth.

Bring your awareness to your hands. Feel any sensation there. You may feel warmth, or tingling, you may feel cold or pain, or maybe even an absence of any sensation. Whatever your experience is, simply allow it to be. Watch it with your attention, don't try to change anything about what you are feeling. All that matters is the sensation, not whether the experience in the hands is good or bad, positive or negative, just the bare experience.

Stay with the feeling in the hands for a while and then if you feel as though your awareness is steady move into the wrists and forearms. Again simply listening to the sensation or the absence of sensation. Stay with those feelings for a while and then gradually move on, letting your awareness move through the rest of your body, up your arms, into your shoulders, up the front of the neck and face and down the back of the head, down through the torso and the back, all the way down the legs into the feet. Take your time to move through the body noting any sensations that you find without judgement. Even if you feel pain try to just feel it as purely a sensation, not as something to be avoided and changed.

If your mind comes in to judge what you are doing, or to comment on the sensation, then allow it do so and then gently come back to the feeling in the body. The mind will not stop thinking, the thoughts are not bad, they too are just a part of life, accept them and then move on. Notice them and allow them to be.

Gradually as you practice this exercise your focus will become stronger. When you feel that you are able to stay with feelings in the body then you can expand your awareness to include any sounds, any smells, the feeling of the air moving. Again just allowing whatever your experiences are to simply be. Not to be judged. This is choiceless awareness. A chance to feel everything inside you and about you in that moment, without judging the experience and sorting it into categories of positive and negative. Just feeling.

In that space of non-judgement we are truly alive, being with whatever comes, accepting all our life, all experience.

## Bínbags anð Blíss

*Let go of your negative feelings as you let go of your rubbish*

Emptying the bin. Yuck! Getting your hands covered in bits of yesterdays dinner and old tomato ketchup, messing around with all that stuff that that you've thrown away, stuff that you thought was out of your life and that you thought you would never have to see again. None of us really like the rubbish, it's rubbish after all.

So, is there a positive amongst all the negatives of our junk?

Yes! Just for a moment consider the reflections on your own life. All of us have things, feelings, thoughts in our lives that we would rather not look at, negatives like anger, jealousy, resentment. Or feelings of self criticism and self judgement that are destructive and harmful to our well-being. All the rubbish that is created in our lives by our reactions to the situations that we find ourselves in. The negatives in our lives are as inevitable as the rubbish in our bins. As there is day, so there is night, if Summer comes we know that Winter is not far behind. It is an undeniable fact of life there are parts of life that are not so pretty, that we would rather not look at.

So what has this got to do with emptying the bin? How does knowing this make an actual difference to the job itself?

Begin by making the connection. The connection between the ugly stuff in your bin and the ugly stuff in your life. Let the act of putting out the rubbish be a significant act.

Pause before you act (just a minute, that's all [you may be surprised how long it feels]) and find something that you no longer want in your life. It may be a feeling that you had that day, perhaps you got angry with someone at work, or the kids have been winding you up like a clockwork toy, or it could be a pattern of thought that is no longer useful to you, maybe you are often hard on yourself or you doubt your own abilities. Then tie that negative to the bin. As you put your household rubbish out of your life, put out the rubbish of the mind. Really touch that negative that you no longer need and let it go. Release it in a final, physical way as you release the physical debris of your life.

You can even use an affirmation as you do this everyday chore. Try saying "I throw away all feelings of ......, right now" as you throw away the rubbish. Using words can make the act much more powerful, it is a physical action that says - I am serious about this! The universe will hear you and help you to fulfil your affirmation.

Who would have thought that putting out the binbags at the end of the day could be an emotional clearing? The act of identifying those things that are not useful to you and sincerely feeling that you are getting rid of them is immensely important. We can try to avoid facing those feelings that bother us and let them pile up like an un-emptied bin or we can consciously let them go from our lives. The job is whatever you want it to be, an empty task that you have to do before you get on with the next thing or a valuable small step in your life.

You can  put out the doubting self when you put out the rest of the rubbish, imagine if every time you emptied your bin you consciously let go of a destructive feeling. Every time. To affirm that you want something to happen, is to make it happen. Don't be afraid, release yourself to be truly free of your inner garbage! Let the bin remind you not to hang onto old and useless feelings. You will always have rubbish come up inside, the debris of the day's feelings. Don't let your inner bin get too full, take the chance to let go of what you no longer need and discover how much lighter you life can be!

## Global Housework

*Personal responsibility and other people's mess*

There is something worse than an enormous pile of dirty dishes, and that's an enormous pile of somebody else's dirty dishes and their nasty greasy mess. When you have made the mess there is always some part of you that knows you are going to have to clean it up. When somebody else made the mess (they don't seem to have that part in them) it takes a different kind of resolution and resignation on your part to set about cleaning it up.

If you have ever shared a house you will know about this. Whether you are sharing your house with your family, your partner or a rugby team tensions will arise. Tensions that are often dismissed as trivial, usually by the person that created them and I quote 'God, what's all the fuss about, its only a bit of washing up'. True it is only a bit of washing up, but it's their washing up, and it is up to them to take care of it. Or so your mind says. Why should I do it, they are his dishes, or her dirty laundry. And so you set about clearing up to the rumbling soundtrack in your head of 'bloody hell, messy bugger, its not fair, I always do all the cleaning', etc, etc, etc.

But if we are talking about responsibility, then what of your responsibility to yourself as you do those resented dishes. What of the responsibility to your body and your well being. Turning you task into an exercise in frustration will send those feelings into your body and it will send those feelings outward. Resentment can easily build between people over these apparently small issues. Tension builds in the house and before long no matter how clean your kitchen surfaces are you are not living in a nice environment.

So how do we avoid these feelings, these tensions? In some ways we never will. Unless you happen to be a fully realised being then thoughts of blame and annoyance will come into your head. It is then that you have the chance to make choice. You can listen to the thoughts and spiral off into a maze of feelings of grumpiness and anger, miss a chunk of you life, miss the chance to melt into the washing up and probably end up taking out your feelings on another person in the house or some unsuspecting passerby. Or you can take a few moments to let go. Watch your thoughts rise then make a conscious choice to let them go, to let the negative feelings sink down into your feet. Make it part of the job, as you begin to wash up for example, allow your hands to rest in the warm water, let any anger dissolve into the warmth, feel your feet and let any heaviness that you feel, whether it be in mind or in body drop down into your feet and be drawn back to the earth. Do you want to feel grumpy?

Of course if you have to do this every day (doing your own chores as well as somebody else's) then it is going to wear a little thin after a while and you will have to take your courage in your hands, address the situation face to face and give up being secretly resentful.

Learning to let go of this resentment is quite a skill. A very important skill at that. We are surrounded by the results of other people's lives and values. By the way in which they live their lives, whether this shows itself in how loud your neighbour plays his stereo, how many cars there are on the road, or in a whole country's beliefs and attitudes. Everywhere and on many levels, (physical, environmental, spiritual, ideological) there are the results of other peoples lives.

Our environment, our beautiful, diverse, life-giving environment is full of other people's mess. There are a lot of chores waiting to be done. We can choose to sit around blaming (its all the fault of the industrial revolution, the USA are to blame etc) or we can let go of that blame and resentment and see what needs to be done. We can change our worlds. Our personal worlds, what immediately surrounds us, the way in which we live our lives and the way in which we feel inside. All we can do is begin from where we are, on a personal level and on a global level there is no time for slinging mud.

Take responsibility for yourself, for your inner world. Take time to enjoy your chores (whatever or whoever's mess you are cleaning), let go of your resentment and feel well. When you feel well inside it spills out, you want your house to feel well, you want your neighbour to feel well and you want you world to feel well. Personal responsibility is global responsibility. Your internal housework can be global housework. The work you do on yourself is work for everyone.

# Tools of the trade

*The tools that we use around the house are as much a part of the house as those things that we are cleaning, they are within it's energy and are respected as we respect the house. They are the physical connectors between us and the house, our medium through which we communicate with the energy. They are made of energy as we are. We have the potential to learn from them, from our tools, if only we can be humble enough to hear what they are saying. Look with fresh eyes and you may see something you have missed, something wonderful, in the object that you have taken for granted...*

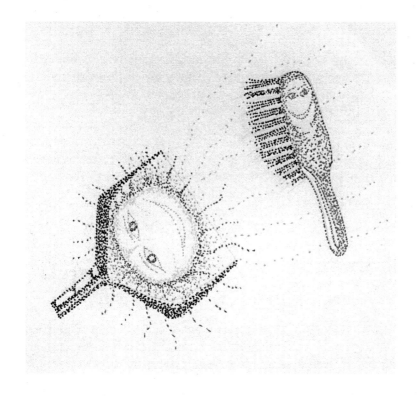

# The Clothes Peg

*Teaching me the creativeness of tension*

An incredibly simple design. Two pieces of plastic and a spring. At one end the plastic is designed to grip, at the other, to be gripped. The spring is a reservoir of energy. There is tension within the metal. It is that stored energy that holds the clothes on the line.

To activate that stored energy you have to use some of your own as a catalyst to begin the process. Feeling the tension and then feeling that tension dissolve as I relax. There will always be tension within the peg, stored in the spring. This is true for you also, there is always energy within you, stored and awaiting release, your tantien, your centre, is the spring where the energy is held.

Look at the peg and work the mechanism to get a feel for what is happening. Surprisingly there is beauty in the design and in the movement. As you press the ends together the pivot action of the peg opens the other end and the opening is lovely, it seems very like the bud of a flower opening, you expend energy and the flower opens, as all flowers need energy to bloom so the peg needs energy to open. The opposite nature of the mechanism means that by creating tension at one end an opening can occur at the other.

This seems apparently contradictory: tension creating relaxation but it is often the same in the human body. We truly appreciate the opening and relaxing feeling of release only when it is preceded by tension, indeed there can be no release without tension.

There is tremendous energy in tension, feel it on a physical level with heat and buzzing in muscles and sinews that are held tightly and also on an emotional level when a feeling fills

you, if you are suddenly very angry then there is enormous tension built inside your body.

We are taught that tension is bad, that what we should look for in our lives is calmness and relaxation. Without tension however then there is no calmness, no opposite. Without clean how can there be dirty? Tension reaches a point of extreme and then transforms into its opposite, relaxation.

The tension holds the energy however, as the spring of the peg holds tension within it, it is when the release comes that the energy is freed and is allowed to move and to create.

Do we pity the poor clothes peg then that only ever enjoys a partial release from tension? No because there will always be a tension within us as there is in the peg. Without tension how would our skin hold our blood within it and how would our bones support our organs. The cycle of tension and release occurs every day in thousands of small ways, when you have a poo, when a sneeze comes, when you feel irritated by something and then dismiss the feeling, and the same cycle is repeated on a far grander scale. In the tension of life and the release of death, in the gathering of lava in a volcano and the release of the eruption, in the birth and death of suns and worlds.

So the humble clothes peg, simple plastic and metal mirrors the events of the universe great and small. Tension and release, conserve and spend. Tension is life, energy is life, the clothes peg contains both and the simple clothes.....

Everything around us is held in it's present form by tension. When tension is totally released then matter returns to energy. We are all energy, everything around us is energy. When we experience release from tension and let go into the stillness of quiet meditation and movement we are experiencing something that is very profound and a mirror of the fundamental principle of life that there are no constants, that we and everything around us is made of energy, of chi. We release and return to chi that is the basis of all things.

So let tension come, let problems and emotions fill me with tension, for within that tension is the possibility of release and ecstasy.

Thank you chi for teaching me that tension can be creative, and thank you to the clothes peg for illustrating it so beautifully. Hanging out the washing may never be the same again!


In Spring's birth, the opening leaf,
A new shoot seeking light's relief,

In the swell of the sea, the curl of the wave,
The hooked bat's foot in the deep, dark cave.

In the predators gaze, or ice and fire,
In the miracle colours of Autumn's pyre

And in words and feelings not expressed,
And people at work becoming stressed

Tension is present in all of life,
Yet tension does not have to mean strife,

And how do we learn of tensions force?
By looking to the peg of course.

## Hanging out (the washing!)

On a glorious Summer day hanging out the washing is a lovely job. Compared to cleaning the toilet most of us would probably agree it is pretty easy, you don't get your hands dirty, you are in the fresh air and you will soon have some lovely clean clothes.

While you are out there, pegs in hand ( wonderful, exciting enlightening pegs!) watch your washing as it flaps about on the line. If you want to learn how to move here is your teacher. If you find stiffness in your back, in your shoulders when you do your housework, when you hang out your washing then it is time to learn about effortless movement from your clothes and the wind.

Just watch for a while, see the wind gently move your clothes, first quietly then with more playfulness. What a privilege to see the wind. Our usually invisible companion reveals himself in the sway of the washing line and the flap of the sheets.

We can learn so much from that movement. Feel yourself being moved by the wind, let your arms hang by your sides and let the wind, even if it is the most gentle breeze, suggest your next movement, allow your self to be guided by the wind. Let go of your thoughts for a while and just return to the simplicity of your body's movement. See how the wind lifts your washing and holds it aloft, let your arm mirror that movement, let it sway and move without trying, without tension.

Feel the winds gentle fingers caress your skin, your arms are moving through air that seems substantial, thick and supportive. Let go of your fears and dance with the wind. It will show you how to move, how to be free. All your tensions dissolve in wonderful release as you dance with your lifelong partner, the wind.

## To Mop or to Mope

Does your housework ever make you feel like giving up?

Do you ever feel like you are attacking your housework?

Find a new way to be, and to be with your mop. Let go all that you know about the mop, all your past experiences of mopping, all that you have got to do with it. It has no meaning in your life, it is an entirely new object, an entirely new task. Anything could happen

## Can you find the spirit in the mop?

If you are very still and just listen for a moment, you may just hear what it is whispering to you...

## The Mop

Wiry growth and twisty, tangled hair

Muddy pools and dirty floors beware.

Shaft of wood and head of string

That clean the outside and within.

I feel in you a gentle power

Friendly warmth and sparkling shower.

I send you down to dirty places

But you return with no ill graces.

So thank you mop, a trusted friend

You show me how to move and bend

As I dance a cleaner's pirouette

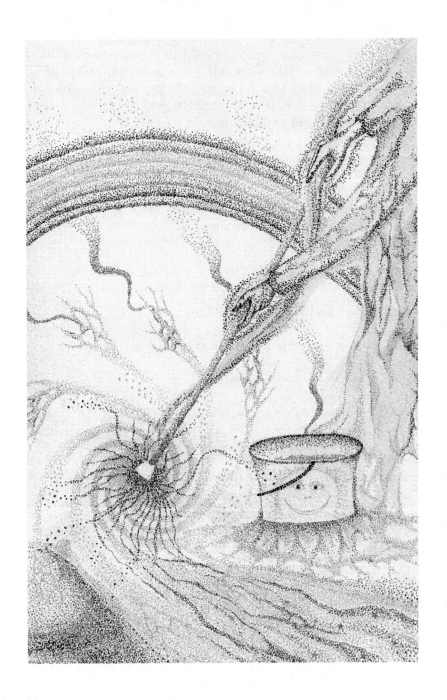

An antidote to all upset.

Your humble form belies your gifts

And the fundamental, heartfelt shifts

That flow to me through your wood handle

My fears and dreams do you untangle.

So sing a praise with all you've got

To the tool of kings, the simple mop.....

# The Sponge Scourer

*The way to the deep down shine*

The sponge scourer is sponge on one side, soft, full of spaces like cells, more space than substance. The other side is hard and abrasive, tough interwoven fibres.

The yin sponge and the Yang scourer, soft receptive sponge and hard and emissive yang scouring surface. I need both properties on my way to the deep down shine. The clarity and focus of the scourer that cleans away confusion and apathy, and the gentleness of the sponge, soft, cleaning balm to draw away the negatives and find the light and shine beneath.

Connect with the sponge. Sit with it upon your open palm. It is so light it is as though it is not even there. The sponge is moulded around the air, containing bubbles, spaces. There is space within it as there is space inside you, inside your lungs, inside your cells. Feel how the energy passes into it and through it.

The boundaries of the sponge are unclear - where does the sponge stop and the air start? The two are joined by spaces. You are connected to all that is about you by spaces. Open your mouth to breathe and air and energy rush in to fill the space inside. There is no boundary between you and what is around you. Like a sponge you absorb - through your mouth, your nose, your skin. You exchange with your environment, you are not a closed organism but a constantly interacting body of chi - emptying and filling, the outside is inside.

You soak up what is around you, light, food, chi, knowledge, words. The more you expose yourself to fresh, new chi the more will be inside of you. Be as a sponge squeeze out the old, tired energies and let in the fresh, clear, revitalising chi.

## To be a Sponge...

Take a pause, a rest from doing. Sit quietly, let your body be alert and balanced. Your spine is upright, not rigid, but gently moving as though there were an invisible golden thread lifting you upwards. Let the breath come and go naturally and gently.

Rest your hands on the floor, palms upwards. Let the earth support them, you need use no effort, your shoulders can relax and drop. Then gently, keeping that feeling of relaxation in your shoulders, arms and hands, raise your arms, palm upwards, towards the sky. You are drawing clear, clean energy up from the earth.

When your palms are above your head, turn them so that the palms face towards your head and the ground. Then let your arms slowly sink down bringing with them fresh, new energy, cleansing and washing your body and your spirit.

Let the exercise clean you like a sponge dipped into clear water. New chi is coming inside you, right now,to flush out all the old tensions, frustrations and negative feelings that you no longer need.

This clearing needs to happen regularly, especially when we have been in stressful situations and soaked up negative energy from what happened around us. As a sponge left too long without rinsing will become stagnant and smelly, so it is with your energy. Let the sponge teach you of exchange and renewal, let it remind you to renew the heart, body, mind and spirit and spiral with new chi.

Choose which side of the sponge scourer to use when you do the exercise. Are you surface cleaning or are you going deeper, releasing old patterns of thought, old grime. Choose how you want to work - a quick shower or a long soak! A swift scour or a full on scrub!

# Beneath the Dirt and Dust...

The dust and crumbs lie thick and cloudy

And hide the shine that clamours loudly

Behind the heavy veils of thought

That cover us and we are caught

Like flies in a web of expectation

Believing there is no relation,

Between us and the sparkling joy of life

That melts and softens internal strife

Until the inner world is wrought

Into a shape beyond all thought

And changes even the simplest chores

Into moves your soul adores.

Please wipe away the dirt and grime

And all the resentment of wasted time

To find  and love a fresh new sparkle

That may surprise and even startle

Your family and friends who see in you

Something green and fresh and new

And shining clean from the dusty past

Your light being home inside at last.

# Hanging with the Vacuum

Something so relied upon, yet so undervalued. We take it out of the cupboard, switch it on, whiz around the floor with it, curse it if it is full and then stick it back into the cupboard.

Poor vacuum! That which gets down into the nitty-gritty of life, picks up and gets rid of all those things that we no longer want or need, discarded crumbs, the dirt from your shoes, the fine waste of our lives. The vacuum accepts them all, welcomes all these particles that we have let go of. I feel like it is time we said a big thank you to the vacuum cleaner, unappreciated servant of the home (and I bet there are a few people out there who have at times thought they were the most unappreciated servant of the home).

Thank you vacuum cleaner for pulling all negatives up your spiral trunk into your hungry belly. The all accepting vacuum. By creating the space inside you, you attract those things that we no longer want in our lives. A reminder then that to deal with the negative feelings and emotions that come to us in the course of our lives we need space. It is in the space that we find clarity. When we can open ourselves and find the space within then negativity disappears into that space. Clarity requires the mind to be as the vacuum, empty and quiet, gently listening. Inside that stillness all negatives, all the dirt of our lives is accepted and in that acceptance made harmless.


Gentle hum and whirr,
When I give you power it is as the breath coming in,
As the breath fills the body with life
So the vacuum breathes into life,
Creating a space inside,

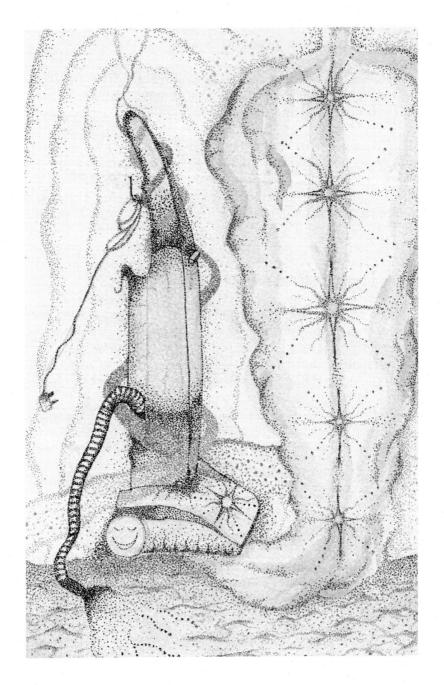

Space gives life to all of us
With space comes clarity, understanding,
Feeling, acceptance
energy
when I listen to the space I hear the sound of energy
of the universe.

## The Dustpan and Brush

*The heart and the mind*

Have you ever given time to wonder about the mind? Do you ever question why it is that you think so many different things every day, that your mind jumps from topic to topic with incredible speed and is sometimes seemingly out of your control? It is the mind that reacts to situations and people and objects that we think we know. When we are faced by something familiar, be that an object, like the mop or a situation that we have faced before our minds immediately jump in to say

"I know that, I've seen that before, that does..." or
"oh, this happened last week, I remember how I felt then, I better feel the same thing this time" or
"I swept the floor yesterday, it wasn't much fun so it will be the same today"

This ability to recognise what we have seen before can be wonderful, it prepares us for life, helps us through day to day situations, without it we would not function too well. Think of a new baby, he or she just lies on its back and the world must seem like a blur of energies, colours, sounds and feelings. The baby hasn't learnt to interpret what it is seeing and fit it into nice neat boxes. Without recognition then we would be overwhelmed by what we saw every day.

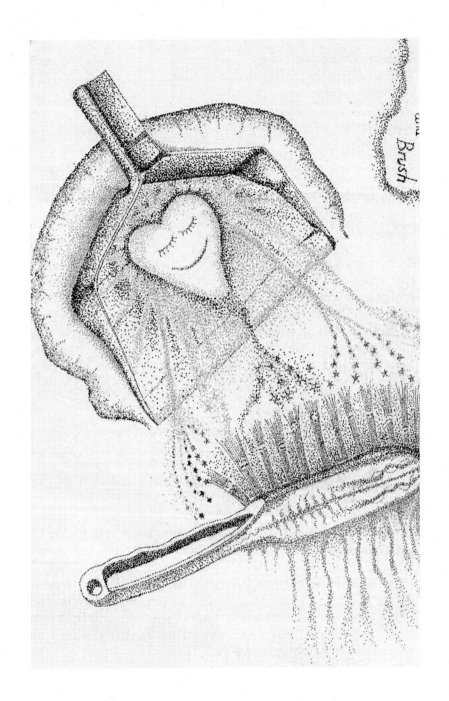

and Brush

But can we find a balance between the wonder of the baby and the child and the understanding of the adult?

Sometimes recognition works against us, it takes away the freshness from situations and things. But it is possible to suspend our reactions for a while.

Have you ever felt that amazing tingle up your spine when you are listening to a piece of music that stirs and moves you, or felt the silent wonder of looking on something that you have never seen before like the sunset that sets the sky on fire in different, rich and wondrous colours every night.

We have the potential to find that feeling in our everyday lives if we can learn to slow down the mind, suspend our recognition for a few moments and see the world as the baby does, with freshness and innocence.

When the mind is quiet, when we stop reacting to the different thoughts and emotions that the mind throws up, something amazing begins to happen.

We begin to feel what is around us, to sense it without thought, just to experience.

The heart comes in to listen, see, smell and feel the world. To really see it, not just to recognise it. The dustpan and brush can teach us how to do this. The heart and the mind are reflected here, and in the reflection we can begin to understand the eternal dance between the heart and the mind.

The brush is the mind, the millions of different thoughts and selves that the mind takes on are reflected in each bristle. When you sweep towards the dustpan you are coming back to yourself, returning to the heart, the essence of you, what is true, what is real.

Feel your breath coming in, the breath going out. In that never ending cycle, the going out and the return, the inhalation and the exhalation is the dance between the heart and the mind, the dustpan and the brush. The brush moves and sways with it's environment, like the mind it is changed by the bumps and contours of life. Life's challenges are uncertain but your true self, your heart, will always be there. That sure beauty remains, always yours to return to.

Release the mind to be as it is, a moving and changing thing, you are returning right now to your true self, to where you came from, to the peace of your heart. As your breath returns to your body so you return to yourself. To the source. To the limitless reservoir of energy inside you that welcomes you back. All your parts, all your selves.

Your heart accepts you as you are, accepts all the dirt and negatives that you sweep in with you. Life's debris is welcomed, not judged. It melts into the energy. You are melting into the energy. You have this wonderful pool of light and energy inside of you right now. Accept. Accept it all, the thousand bristles, the thousand selves. Return to yourself, feel the solidity and the strength that are there now. Feel the beauty of coming home to yourself, to the essential core of you.

Let go of the pressure of what is around you, that which your brush sweeps daily, let your mind be as it is, a moving and changing thing, there will always be more dirt to sweep over, let it go for now, release the tasks of the mind. You are returning to what is real, the love of your heart that accepts you, totally as you are. Let the separateness melt away. You are whole again, complete.

There will always be the dance between the heart and the mind. Both are part of this amazing life. Accept the movement between the two, the going out and the return to the heart, the sweeping of the brush ad the return to unity. You are whole, melt into life's energy and be blessed.

59

# Cínɗerella

*In which our ordinary workaday heroine discovers something new about her sink, falls head over heels in love and shuts the door on Prince Charming.*

## Cínɗerella

Once upon a time there was a girl called Cinderella. She was as normal as you or I, she lived in medium sized terraced house in a medium sized town and worked in a medium sized job. Cinderella had a little boy and nobody to help her look after him so when she came home from work she was always busy taking care of him. It wasn't always an easy job! If any of you know little boys then you will know that what they are really good at are two things, getting into trouble and making

a mess. Now James, for that was his name, was no exception.

In fact if there was ever a prize awarded for messy boys then James's name would be pretty close to the top of the list. Poor Cinderella sometimes felt that there were not enough hours in her day to take care of all the things that needed doing, all the crisps that needed to be vacuumed off the carpet, all the dishes that needed to be cleaned, all the parts of her house that needed to be polished, dusted, wiped and washed.

Some days she would wish that her fairy Godmother would arrive, wave her magic wand at all the chores and turn Cinderella into a rich and beautiful lady of leisure, or that

prince charming would knock on the door and whisk her away to a romantic and far off land. Sometimes she just felt so tired out by the hundreds of little jobs that she had to do each and every day that she would pray for just a little bit more space and time in her life for her, just for her.

Then one day when Cinders was standing at the sink, dishes piled up to her ears, James swinging on the hem of her skirt and a small mountain of dirty clothes wobbling behind her she felt something strange happening. There was a warm tingling sensation dancing around her fingers and hands in the washing up bowl. It was a beautiful feeling of vibrancy and aliveness.

Well Cinders was so surprised that she immediately took her hands out of the water and peered at them closely.

They looked the same, soapy and a little bit wrinkled by the water, but more hers somehow. They weren't just things on

the ends of her arms for doing the washing up with but they really and truly belonged to her, they felt warm and alive and connected to the rest of her body. She gazed at her hands in wonder, moving her fingers very gently and being aware of every tiny movement that she made. The feeling got a little stronger and she felt it in her wrists too.

That was too much for Cinders, her mind came in to analyse what she was feeling, 'don't be silly just get on with the washing up, you've got a million and one things to do' and 'that water must have been a little hot'. And then the feeling was gone and she was just doing the washing up again.

Cinderella quickly forgot about how her hands had felt, the clothes needed ironing and James had to get ready for school, there was just too much to do to stand around enjoying waving her fingers about over the washing up bowl. That night though as she finally lay in bed and breathed a sigh of relief she remembered that feeling and how lovely it was, it had seemed almost magic.

What had she been doing to make it happen? Then she remembered that while she was doing the washing up that time she had just stopped for a second and felt how lovely and gentle and warm the water felt. This was not a usual feeling by any means, usually she just got on with what she had to do and got it done as quickly as possible so that she might get five minutes to sit down afterwards. But this time through that feeling of being in a hurry had been a sense of letting go into the water. Cinders remembered how lovely the water had felt and then how her hands had tingled and how for just that short time she hadn't felt fed up or tired or hurried and a big smile spread across her face in bed.

Feeling a little bit silly and nervous she crept downstairs, being careful to be quiet and not wake up the snoring James, she made her way down to the kitchen and the sink. She

stopped and looked at the sink. It looked different now, in the night, when all the washing up had been done and all the plates put away and rather than feeling resigned to having to do yet more washing up Cinderella felt wide awake and quite excited. A little voice cropped up in her head and said 'what are you doing, go back to bed and stop being so silly' but she ignored it and as if to reassure her she felt a little tingling in her fingers as she approached the sink. It was as though, by the simple fact of approaching her own sink that she had stood at thousands of times before, with a new intention, a fresh acceptance she had transformed something run of the mill and familiar into something exciting and energising. The tingle came again. She wasn't even washing up and she was feeling the tingling. What was going on?

Cinders turned on the tap feeling almost naughty to be playing with the sink in the middle of the night. She glanced behind her sure for a moment  that someone was watching her even though she knew that no-one could be, she just felt a little embarrassed. She pushed the feeling away and turned the tap.

Water gushed forth as always, but this time she saw the bubbles appear and dance about the polished steel of the sink, she saw the spiral of the water in the sink, the flow as it span down the plug hole. Why had she never seen this before, she felt she was seeing something beautiful, something special. Part of Cinders was still saying 'it's only the sink you silly girl, what's so special about that?' but the stronger part of Cinders knew better, she knew that she was seeing the beauty that was always there but that she had never been slow enough to see before. She was looking with child's eyes. With the eyes of wonder.

Suddenly Cinderella was tremendously excited about doing the washing up, about actually putting her hands into that

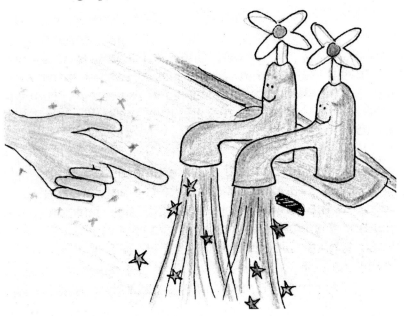

sink, with all its beautiful reflections and dancing water. She couldn't imagine anything she would rather be doing than putting her hands into that sink, under that miniature waterfall and, moving closer, she began to move her hands under the cascade of water, as though she were washing up. One hand held the imaginary plate and the other moved the sponge. Slowly ever so slowly she moved, millimetre by millimetre, sensing every tiny movement, feeling her fingers, her hands, her arms.

The energy was there again, that tingling feeling dancing over her hands. With a sense of joy she felt herself melt into that warm alive energy, and the more she allowed herself to melt, the further the feeling spread until it was all about her arms, her face softened and opened and if she could have looked at herself then she would have seen a gentle light in her eyes and a youthfulness in her skin that she thought had passed many years ago.

She began to move her whole body with her hands, she felt how her arms and elbows were guided by her tummy, her legs were soft and fluid and her feet seemed to be rooted in the ground. Cinderella was alive with joy, she somehow felt that she was coming home to a place that she had never been before but that was more familiar and safe than even her own bedroom.

She never knew how long she stood there for that night, it may have been an hour or as little as ten minutes, but when at last she stepped back from the sink and made her way back upstairs to bed she felt like somebody new, someone with a secret.

The next day dawned as usual with a list of things that had to be done running through Cinderella's head. Packed lunches, washing, ironing, perhaps a spot of vacuuming. She bashed the alarm clock and stumbled downstairs to face that bit of

vacuuming that hadn't got done the night before. There was the vacuum waiting for her as usual and she plugged it in and was about to switch it on when suddenly she stopped, stock still. The sink, she remembered the sink, it wasn't a dream at all.

She felt like dashing in to the kitchen to see if it was real. But then she realised what she was looking at, the vacuum. If she had seen so much wonder in the sink the night before was it possible that it was there in the vacuum too? But how to find it? How to find those child's eyes again. Cinders remembered the slow way she had moved last night and she stopped what she was doing and just stood there, not moving. She felt the criticising voices come up again but, more familiar with them now, she just let them drift off and concentrated on her slowness. The tingling feeling started at her feet this time and she new that what she had felt last night was real and that she could find it again. With a smile, she began to vacuum.

James woke up at about the same time as usual and rubbed the sleepy dust from his eyes. Grabbing his favourite toy he wandered down stairs and opened the door to the lounge. Now as a little boy James was used to some strange sights, but this was a new one on him, his mum was dancing with the vacuum. She had a great big smile on her face, a funny look in her eye and she was definitely dancing with the vacuum. The pot plants were wobbling slightly and the cat was nowhere to be seen but she certainly looked happy.

Being a small boy James looked for about thirty seconds then shrugged and got on with whatever it is that little boys do in the morning when they should be eating their breakfast and doing their teeth. Cinderella danced around him, smiling, vacuuming and tingling with energy and excitement.

Things are different now for Cinderella. She still has loads to do, loads of housework, loads of work work and a little boy who is trying for the naughtiest boy in the world cup. She smiles more though and at funny things. She doesn't wish for a fairy Godmother anymore, she feels like her fairy godmother is pretty much living with her full time and working some pretty unusual magic spells. Every day she falls more in love with her house. With her mop, her J-cloth, her iron. Doing the chores is not such a chore.

Sometimes she catches herself getting into a tizzy about how much she has got to do and then she just stops, stops for about a minute or so until a smile starts to come to her face and then she begins again only a little slower this time and with more feeling. Housework has stopped being housework and become house care, house healing, house love. And Cinderella is looking and feeling better too, she moves more easily, her face is softer and she feels clean inside. As the months went by and she practised what she had learnt she felt more and more energy, more and more peaceful and more and more accepting of the endless housework she faced.

Then one day while she was drifting back and forth with the iron, loving the motion, feeling a stirring in her belly and a tingling round her body, there came a knock on the door. Cinderella put down her iron with a little internal thank you and went to the door. She pulled the door wide and saw on the step a beautiful man who held in his hand a glass slipper.

"You shall go to the ball, Cinderella" he said in a voice like plush velvet curtains, and he held out the slipper.

"No thanks" said Cinderella"I'm doing the ironing"

and with a small smile she closed the door.

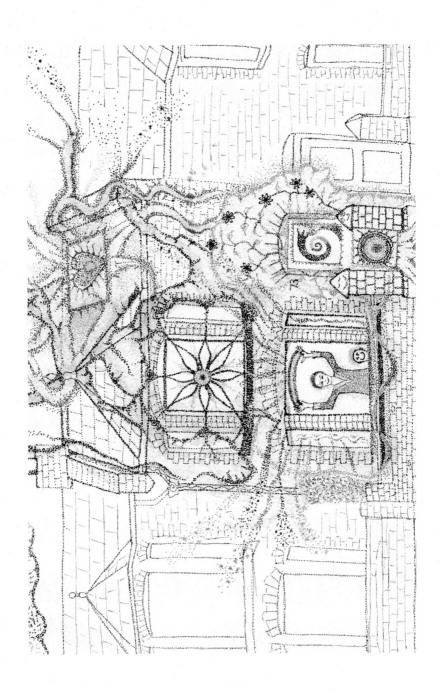

## A Note on Fairy Tales

The ultimate transformation through housework must be Cinderella who slaves away with the mop and bucket, the kitchen stove and the broom, all for the sake of her sisters. And what humbleness she finds in her tasks. In the end it is through her humbleness that she finds her transformation. Her fairy Godmother appears to help her find her dream, and she appears because of Cinderella's goodness and humility. In her quiet devotion to the simple tasks of the house she finds her light, and it is a light from inside all the fairy Godmother does is point it out to her.

O.K., O.K. I know it is just a story, and that the fairy godmother showers Cinders with riches and chariots and glass slippers, but there is great deal of truth here also. There really can be transformation in the humbleness of the household task. In gentle acceptance of the work, in quiet attention and peaceful enjoyment you will find the light inside you. Your fairy Godmother will arrive to whisk you off to a ball more wonderful than in any fairy tale, the fabulous dance of your heart. Your prince Charming is inside of you right now. He is offering you the glass slipper and on the bottom in small letters is written, housework, one size fits all.

So listen, can you hear it? That sound is the chance to feel refreshed and renewed every day, a chance to turn the pumpkin into a beautiful carriage. Slow down and turn your ear to the call of your heart calling on you to trust and to love. To be alive, wholly alive and accept your life. You have the magic wand, it is only a question of slowing down enough to use it. Transform your life, you have the power, it is your choice....

# A Final Word

# The Patience of Growth

*The gentle art of allowing change to come*

There is no instant fix, no giant leaps. You won't suddenly pick up a dustpan and brush and feel full of glowing light and energy. Your house won't be transformed into a rainbow fountain after one whip round with the vacuum. And yes there are days when doing the chores will be the last thing that you want to be doing.

But take small steps, gentle steps, inch by inch move forwards. If you use the exercises in the book, take time to listen to yourself and find space and don't expect too much too quickly then something wonderful will happen. Trust the process and let change come, as inner change always comes, quietly and gradually.

You can't hurry the process by wanting it more or even by trying harder, indeed sometimes it is when you stop trying that you will begin to experience energy. Persistent and constant effort with the exercises, reminding yourself to slow down and listen will yield results. As you learn to slow down and feel the moment also slow down your expectations. You will find it hard sometimes, and sometimes you will find it beautifully easy. If you stop placing high and unrealistic expectations of dramatic shifts in yourself then you will find the gentle and tiny steps wonderful in themselves.

Enjoy each one, don't worry where you are going or how long it will take to get there, be with the going and love the slow and gentle revelation of new paths inside yourself. Like your housework this journey will go on forever, and like your housework when you listen to where you are right now and let go of what might come and how quickly it will be here then you will discover the joy in quiet moments and quiet movements.

Do you want to feel all the love in your life right now, to have one blinding moment of inspiration or would you rather enjoy a beautiful and gentle feeling every day? Would you want to eat all the food you will ever eat in one enormous meal? or would you rather enjoy tastes and smells every day.

Feel love every day as you move about your house, through your daily tasks. Feel love every day on your journey through your life, back home, back to your true self. When you are quiet, when the mind is still you may just hear the sound inside. The gentle call of your true self beckoning you home... Home inside, where home has always been, where it always will be.

*Every step is more precious than gold*
*Every step is full of grace*
*Don't run, just slow down*
*and listen....*
*for each footfall*
*echoes the heartbeat of the universe.*

# A Journey's Tale

Well, I've written a book about housework, I wouldn't have believed it possible. It is sometimes said that everyone has a book inside them, I always thought that mine might have been about high adventure and glorious deeds. I imagined firm jawed heroes and beautiful ladies, instead I got dirty cupboards and sponge scourers. But thank goodness! Something real! Something important.

Everyone does housework at one time or another, more or less often depending on how you like to live. We all have to wash the dishes, clean the toilet and generally spend some time getting down and dirty. Not many of us are firm jawed enough to leap tall buildings in a single bound, rescue damsels from great distress etc etc. So I'm glad, Glad to have written a book that we can all relate to in one way or another.

It has been a challenging, wonderful, difficult, blissful, bubbly, soapy journey. I have learnt as I have written. When I began housework was just another must do, something to get out of the way. But as the words have come, as the experiences have come, as the energy has come it has changed for me, evolved. Evolved into something new, a new mirror to know myself, a new way to feel and to love my life, a new chance to slow down and see the reality of the universe in everything that we do, everything that we touch.

We are beings of energy, of light. We see a limited world and our limited form. But there can be times when this melts away and what we are left with is a beautiful, formless glimpse of what reality really is. I have known this with my mind for a long time, even the physicists told me it was true but I never would have guessed I could see it in the sink! I expected that maybe such things would be revealed to me if I spent years wrapped only in a loin cloth meditating on top of a mountain, depriving myself and otherwise being ever so holy and spiritual. But the truth is here now! All around you, in the pages of the book, in the seat you are sitting on, in your dirty washing. And most of all, inside you.

This book is one way to look at it and to look within, an encouragement to step sideways just a little and look at reality a little differently, to defy your limitations and blow a big raspberry at the mind that thinks it knows this world, that thinks there are no surprises anymore. I know differently, I feel differently. There is so much joy in the world, in you. If you slow down and listen you may hear it. If you slow down and feel you may feel it. Look with new eyes and you may just see it, a glimpse is all you need to know what is true and after that glimpse nothing, no thing, will ever be the same again.

So take heart, take courage, defy your limitations and discover a most beautiful new country, a beautiful new world. You need not journey many miles, travel many leagues, for what you seek is already here, already inside you. Just return, return to your true self, return to you.

## Acknowledgements

I feel so much gratitude for where I am, for what I have written, and I need to direct that gratitude around the place to some special people.

So thank you Choy and Rainbow Tai-chi for showing me what if possible, for guidance, for advice and for untold inspiration. You have shown me how to change my world,

And thank you to Bo and James my fairy tale friends who bless me daily with their gifts of love (and patience).

And to Sarah, John and Jake who gave me the space to write this and (confession time) helped me with my housework when I was too busy writing about it to do it.

The wonderful photos are by Amy who's help really got things moving along and without whom it would have been an empty book.

Thank you Maharaji for countless beautiful reminders of simplicity and the power of the heart.

And to the mop, the sink, the dustpan and brush, the sponge scourer, the clothes peg and all the other wonderful objects in and around my house - I couldn't have done it without you!

Wow, so much and so many people to be grateful to. And that is only a few of them. It has been quite a journey and I would have been lost without my friends and teachers to point the way.

# FREE DETAILED CATALOGUE

Capall Bann is owned and run by people actively involved in many of the areas in which we publish. A detailed illustrated catalogue is available on request, SAE or International Postal Coupon appreciated. **Titles can be ordered direct from Capall Bann, post free in the UK** (cheque or PO with order) or from good bookshops and specialist outlets.

Do contact us for details on the latest releases at: **Capall Bann Publishing, Auton Farm, Milverton, Somerset, TA4 1NE.** Titles include:

A Breath Behind Time, Terri Hector
Arthur - The Legend Unveiled, C Johnson & E Lung
Astrology The Inner Eye - A Guide in Everyday Language, E Smith
Auguries and Omens - The Magical Lore of Birds, Yvonne Aburrow
Asyniur - Womens Mysteries in the Northern Tradition, S McGrath
Beginnings - Geomancy, Builder's Rites & Electional Astrology in the
        European Tradition, Nigel Pennick
Between Earth and Sky, Julia Day
Book of the Veil , Peter Paddon
Caer Sidhe - Celtic Astrology and Astronomy, Vol 1, Michael Bayley
Call of the Horned Piper, Nigel Jackson
Cat's Company, Ann Walker
Celtic Faery Shamanism, Catrin James
Celtic Faery Shamanism - The Wisdom of the Otherworld, Catrin James
Celtic Lore & Druidic Ritual, Rhiannon Ryall
Celtic Sacrifice - Pre Christian Ritual & Religion, Marion Pearce
Celtic Saints and the Glastonbury Zodiac, Mary Caine
Crystal Clear - A Guide to Quartz Crystal, Jennifer Dent
Crystal Doorways, Simon & Sue Lilly
Crossing the Borderlines - Guising, Masking & Ritual Animal Disguise in the
        European Tradition, Nigel Pennick
Dragons of the West, Nigel Pennick
Earth Dance - A Year of Pagan Rituals, Jan Brodie
Earth Harmony - Places of Power, Holiness & Healing, Nigel Pennick
Earth Magic, Margaret McArthur
Enchanted Forest - The Magical Lore of Trees, Yvonne Aburrow
Eternal Priestess, Sage Weston
Eternally Yours Faithfully, Roy Radford & Evelyn Gregory
Everything You Always Wanted To Know About Your Body, But So Far
        Nobody's Been Able To Tell You, Chris Thomas & D Baker
Fairies in the Irish Tradition, Molly Gowen

Familiars - Animal Powers of Britain, Anna Franklin
Fool's First Steps, (The) Chris Thomas
Forest Paths - Tree Divination, Brian Harrison, Ill. S. Rouse
From Past to Future Life, Dr Roger Webber
Gardening For Wildlife Ron Wilson
God Year, The, Nigel Pennick & Helen Field
Goddess on the Cross, Dr George Young
Goddess Year, The, Nigel Pennick & Helen Field
Goddesses, Guardians & Groves, Jack Gale
Handbook For Pagan Healers, Liz Joan
Handbook of Fairies, Ronan Coghlan
Healing Book, The, Chris Thomas and Diane Baker
Healing Homes, Jennifer Dent
Healing Journeys, Paul Williamson
Healing Stones, Sue Philips
Herb Craft - Shamanic & Ritual Use of Herbs, Lavender & Franklin
In Search of Herne the Hunter, Eric Fitch
Intuitive Journey, Ann Walker Isis - African Queen, Akkadia Ford
Language of the Psycards, Berenice
Legend of Robin Hood, The, Richard Rutherford-Moore
Lid Off the Cauldron, Patricia Crowther
Light From the Shadows - Modern Traditional Witchcraft, Gwyn
Lore of the Sacred Horse, Marion Davies
Lost Lands & Sunken Cities (2nd ed.), Nigel Pennick
Magic of Herbs - A Complete Home Herbal, Rhiannon Ryall
Magical Guardians - Exploring the Spirit and Nature of Trees, Philip Heselton
Magical History of the Horse, Janet Farrar & Virginia Russell
Magical Lore of Animals, Yvonne Aburrow
Magical Lore of Cats, Marion Davies
Magical Lore of Herbs, Marion Davies
Magick Without Peers, Ariadne Rainbird & David Rankine
Medium Rare - Reminiscences of a Clairvoyant, Muriel Renard
Menopausal Woman on the Run, Jaki da Costa
Mind Massage - 60 Creative Visualisations, Marlene Maundrill
Moon Mysteries, Jan Brodie
Mysteries of the Runes, Michael Howard
Mystic Life of Animals, Ann Walker
Pagan Feasts - Seasonal Food for the 8 Festivals, Franklin & Phillips
Patchwork of Magic - Living in a Pagan World, Julia Day
Pathworking - A Practical Book of Guided Meditations, Pete Jennings
Personal Power, Anna Franklin
Pillars of Tubal Cain, Nigel Jackson
Practical Divining, Richard Foord
Practical Meditation, Steve Hounsome
Practical Spirituality, Steve Hounsome
Psychic Self Defence - Real Solutions, Jan Brodie

Real Fairies, David Tame
Reality - How It Works & Why It Mostly Doesn't, Rik Dent
Romany Tapestry, Michael Houghton
Runic Astrology, Nigel Pennick
Sacred Animals, Gordon MacLellan
Sacred Celtic Animals, Marion Davies, Ill. Simon Rouse
Sacred Dorset - On the Path of the Dragon, Peter Knight
Sacred Grove - The Mysteries of the Forest, Yvonne Aburrow
Sacred Geometry, Nigel Pennick
Sacred Nature, Ancient Wisdom & Modern Meanings, A Cooper
Sacred Ring - Pagan Origins of British Folk Festivals, M. Howard
Season of Sorcery - On Becoming a Wisewoman, Poppy Palin
Seasonal Magic - Diary of a Village Witch, Paddy Slade
Secret Places of the Goddess, Philip Heselton
Secret Signs & Sigils, Nigel Pennick
Self Enlightenment, Mayan O'Brien
Spirits of the Earth, Jaq D Hawkins
Stumbling Through the Undergrowth , Mark Kirwan-Heyhoe
Subterranean Kingdom, The, revised 2nd ed, Nigel Pennick
Symbols of Ancient Gods, Rhiannon Ryall
Talking to the Earth, Gordon MacLellan
Taming the Wolf - Full Moon Meditations, Steve Hounsome
Teachings of the Wisewomen, Rhiannon Ryall
Tree: Essence, Spirit & Teacher, Simon & Sue Lilly
Through the Veil, Peter Paddon
Torch and the Spear, Patrick Regan
Understanding Chaos Magic, Jaq D Hawkins
Warp and Weft - In Search of the I-Ching, William de Fancourt
Way of the Magus, Michael Howard
Weaving a Web of Magic, Rhiannon Ryall
West Country Wicca, Rhiannon Ryall
Wildwitch - The Craft of the Natural Psychic, Poppy Palin
Wildwood King , Philip Kane
Wondrous Land - The Faery Faith of Ireland by Dr Kay Mullin
Working With the Merlin, Geoff Hughes
Your Talking Pet, Ann Walker

# FREE detailed catalogue and FREE 'Inspiration' magazine

## Contact: Capall Bann Publishing, Auton Farm, Milverton, Somerset, TA4 1NE